S0-AXR-044

For My Daughter, My Friend

LIDIA MARIA RIBA

Bristol Park Books

Copyright © 2010 by Lidia Maria Riba
Copyright © 2010 V & R Editoras

www.vreditoras.com

All rights reserved. No part of this work may be reproduced or transmitted in any form or by any means, electronic or mechanical, including photocopying, recording, or any information storage and retrieval system without permission in writing from the publisher.

The illustration credits on page 80 constitute an extension of the copyright page.

Bristol Park Books
252 West 38th Street
New York, NY 10018

Bristol Park Books is a registered trademark
of Bristol Park Books, Inc.

Library of Congress Control Number: 2016959780

ISBN: 978-0-88486-641-1

E-Book ISBN: 978-0-88486-642-8

Text and cover design by Keira McGuinness
Cover art copyright © 2016 Danussa/Shutterstock

Printed in Malaysia

TO

_____

FROM

_____

The strongest, deepest feeling came over me when I held you against my heart for the first time. That feeling was: I want to give. Give you life. Give you warmth. Give you security...that feeling has stayed with me as we've grown up together. I wanted to give you all of the best in the world. The sun, the stars, and the moon...

But I am just a mother. During those first years, I was your shield, your angel, and your fairy godmother. But today, the paths open before you and I must let you go. And I give you my word. I will always be with you, to help you to make you smile. I will tell you stories, I will thank you, I will ask for forgiveness and I will remember our good and our bad times…all to celebrate the wonder of being your mother and having you, my daughter.

With love,

Mom

About
Mothers &
Daughters

What woman hasn't dreamed of fame and glory? To be accepting the Nobel Prize; to be a famous actress receiving her Oscar in front of thousands; to hit the highest note of *La Traviata*...

And God, with a complicit wink, gave women an additional gift: the astonishing ability to create, not a masterpiece of literature, not a scientific discovery, but the incomparable work of art that is a daughter's smile.

Few images in the world are as powerful as looking into the mirror next to a teenage daughter all dressed up for her first date. Oh! How fast has time flown by...

And there's a secret pride in a mother's smile when her friend says, "I just spoke with your daughter and thought she was you: you two sound exactly alike!"

I overheard you talking to your best friend about something that was bothering you, something I had no idea about. I was a little surprised, and a little sad. I thought : now you have your own world, which I can only enter if you let me.

My friends who have only boys brag about their special relationship. But what do they know of the excitement of your first party dress? Or of the complexity of sharing make-up, of the closeness of our souls when we both cry at the same movie?

How can they imagine my relief when after you mercilessly analyze my new dress you pronounce, "It looks good, Mom." There is no harsher judge than my daughter; nor a more sincere opinion than that of my daughter. That's why I value your compliments so.

If our house ever caught on fire, I would try to save the little clay jar you painted all by yourself when you were seven years old. Nothing in the world could ever replace it. Those small and precious things from you, more than anything else, would help us make a new home.

During an argument, when I see your beloved face contorted with rage as you yell,

"There's no use talking to you. You don't understand anything!"

I close my eyes and imagine the photos in my family album, Where did those astonished eyes go? Those outreached hands? The perfectly combed hair I used to fix? I open my eyes and see, yes, it's all there, hidden behind youthful rebellion.

I sigh... and patiently keep listening.

I WISH
I COULD
PROTECT
YOU

... from the false words of someone who claims to be your friend; from the unfair grade on the exam you studied so hard for; from the rain on the day of that very special picnic; from you ever having to go on a diet; from putting your faith in something or someone that disappoints you; from loving the wrong guy (not because I don't like him, but because he can't make you happy); from getting hurt or suffering; from your favourite dress being at the dry cleaner's on the day he asks you out; from extreme cold and heat; from storms and hurricanes. But I can't. So, I am opening the door and telling you: live your own life.

There was a time
in my life when
I thought I had
everything

Youth, romance, work I loved, travel, friends…and then you arrived. And I understood the meaning of the word: fulfillment. Today, I don't care that I don't have everything. I have you. That's more than enough.

I always wanted to be a bastion of fortitude

a beacon to guide you toward your destiny. However sometimes this tower leans and everything around me grows dark. Then with your hand on my shoulder and your comforting words, I am not alone and light returns.

If mothers could share with their daughters just twenty percent of what we think of them, their self-esteem would be indestructible.

TAKE
ME
WITH
YOU

Back to school and playtime; to rambunctious birthday parties with chocolate cake; to secrets with your best friends, and to your sports tournaments.

Take me with you to the anticipation of your first date and the sadness of your first disappointment.

Take me with you to college, and sleepless nights studying and dreaming; to climb that mountain or to catch the waves on your surf board; to the excitement as the curtain rises on your play and the applause of professors on hearing your doctoral thesis.

Take me with you on your photography safari and the ecstasy of seeing a painting by Monet.

Take me with you in your heart wherever you go.

I
WANT

ou to discover that the best things in this world do not carry a price but do have great value; a dew drop on a rose in the morning; the words "I'm sorry." Sunsets at the beach, a baby's hand squeezing yours, that moment when, yes, it's him on the phone, times when a storm bangs against the windows, and the words, "thank you."

I want daybreak

To surprise you,

as you are talking with friends

about fixing the world,

passionately arguing

about what

you believe in.

I want you to never grow up entirely. To keep innocence in your heart and to believe that sometimes the world really can be magical, that not every just cause is doomed, and that there are days when dawn seems to break twice.

I don't want you to be bitter or sceptical
if someone wounds you deeply.
I wish I could shield you.
Rise up again from the ashes!
Confront the challenge. Do not give up.
Don't be persuaded that everything lets
you down.
Lift your gaze. Look at the horizon...
and believe.

I want you to have
the strong, deep,
unwavering love of
a great man. And
I want you to enjoy it
for your life.

And I want you to experience

the craziness, the overwhelming

passion, that may transport you through

heaven and hell.

May you live it fully...and then be able

to let it go.

I pray that you will always have faith in God. Imagine him however you wish, or however you can, but look for him. Look around and you will find that he is always present.

I want you to discover the pleasure of reading; the intoxicating sensation of living for a few hours with the characters of a novel; the possibility of forgetting your worries and sorrows; escaping to another time or some foreign land.

And I wish for you to feel the deep emotion of poetry. May your spirit be touched as you discover that precise word that expresses what you feel.

Thank You

... for all the birthday cards, Mother's Day cards, and notes found under my pillow, calling me the "best mother in the world."

No music can ever
sound so good as
your sweet words.

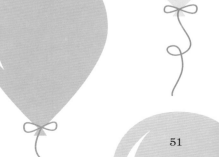

And thank you for being so different

from what I had imagined;

unique, extraordinary,

AND MUCH BETTER THAN I COULD HAVE DREAMED

Thank you for telling me about

that wonderful party.

I'll never forget

your bright eyes,

your unstoppable enthusiasm,

your hands waving in the air,

just so you could share it with me.

Nothing has taught me as much

about my own life

as trying to teach you:

glimpsing my own faults,

while in the midst of a solemn

lecture to you.

I tried to improve.

Thank you.

I

Forgive

You

For wanting to leave home when you were six, threatening to trade me in for another mother, "Any other mother!" were your exact words. And I was so relieved when, just half an hour later, you decided to stay and to accept me the way was.

FORGIVE ME

For all the times I wanted you to be first in your class, prima ballerina, professional tennis player. At some point, I guess, I vainly believed that my daughter was a second chance for me to achieve what I didn't.

you have shown me that my own expectations could never match the joys of your reality.

I have a long list
in my heart of things
I should have done with
you and for you

Sometimes I wonder

if you have in your heart

a short list of the things I did do?

I wanted to be a rock

of solid principles

to educate my children.

It was so easy in the beginning.

But then you started growing up

and noticing my flaws. You heard me lie

about my age, and you found that

candy bar wrapper after I swore to you

that I was on a very strict diet.

And all the while I was preaching to

you about truth, and honesty.

Thank you for

your wise and kind

forgiveness

REMEMBER

You might have some special talent. But talents vanish into fantasies without practice and perseverance... which is completely up to you.

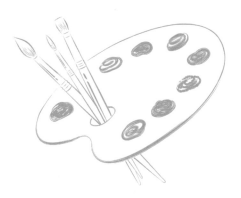

If you want to chase the rainbow,

do it. Most importantly,

enjoy every stretch of the road

 that takes you there.

Planning for a trip, an event, a party

is almost always more fun that the

event itself.

Find the time to plan what will make

you happy.

Recipes for happiness are simple: laugh a lot (especially at yourself) and love a lot. Love your friends, your work, the person with whom you will share your life, nature that surrounds and sustains you...and your mother, of course, your mother.

The boldest, most altruistic intentions don't equal the smallest action. Even if you can't do the best, do something.

Look for your roots. Seek out your history. So many people gave of themselves so that you could be the person you are. Their talents, their passions may be realized through you. All of us who love you see something of ourselves in you. You are your yesterday as well as today's self. Unique. Magnificent.

I

LOVE

YOU

Illustration Credits

pp 1, 3, images copyright © Danussa/Shutterstock

pp 6, 20, 23, images copyright © etcberry/Shutterstock

pp 8–9, 14, 16 images copyright © Sopelkin/Shutterstock

pp 10–11, image copyright © vareika tamara/Shutterstock

pp 12–13, image copyright © Macrovector/Shutterstock

p 15, image copyright © Natasha R. Graham/Shutterstock

p 18, image copyright © Mitar Vidakovic/Shutterstock

p 25, image copyright © mashabr/Shutterstock

p 27, image copyright © En min Shen/Shutterstock

p 28, image copyright © Transia Design/Shutterstock

p 30, image copyright © Betelgejze/Shutterstock

p 31, image copyright © HelenField/Shutterstock

p 32, image copyright © Baleika Tamara/Shutterstock

pp 33, 37, 38–39, images copyright © silm/Shutterstock

p 34, image copyright © mirrelleyt/Shutterstock

p 41, image copyright © Anikei/Shutterstock

p 42, image copyright © TsipiLevin/Shutterstock

p 45, image copyright © sunshiny/Shutterstock

p 46, image copyright © Talirina/Shutterstock

p 48, image copyright © sharpner/Shutterstock

pp 49, 54, images copyright © Nataliva/Shutterstock

pp 50–51, images copyright © Erinphoto10/Shutterstock

p 52, image copyright © AnnaSimo/Shutterstock

p 53, image copyright © EYE-Q/Shutterstock

p 56, image copyright © milksilk/Shutterstock

pp 58–59, images copyright © Anettphoto/Shutterstock

pp 60–61, images copyright © Veronique G/Shutterstock

p 62, image copyright © Annie Dove/Shutterstock

p 63, image copyright © Natalia_ngr/Shutterstock

p 64, image copyright © natsa/Shutterstock

p 66, image copyright © Pikovit/Shutterstock

p 68, image copyright © Olga Hmelevskaya/Shutterstock

p 69, images copyright © Texturis/Shutterstock

p 70, image copyright © An Vino/Shutterstock

p 71, image copyright © Sonya illustration/Shutterstock

pp 72–73, images copyright © blue67design/Shutterstock

pp 74–75, images copyright © kirate/Shutterstock

p 7, image copyright © Daria Rosen/Shutterstock

p 79, image copyright © NMarty/Shutterstock

endpapers, image copyright © Transia Design/Shutterstock